Funeral

Church House Publishing

Published by   Church House Publishing
                Church House
                Great Smith Street
                London SW1P 3NZ

Copyright ©   *The Archbishops' Council 2000*

                First published 2000

                0 7151 2039 5 (standard format)
                0 7151 2040 9 (large format)

Printed and bound by ArklePrint Ltd, Northampton
on 80 gsm Dutchman Ivory

Typeset in Gill Sans
by John Morgan and Shirley Thompson/Omnific
Designed by Derek Birdsall RDI

The material in this booklet is extracted from *Common Worship: Pastoral Services*. It comprises:

¶   The Outline Order for Funerals;
¶   The Funeral Service;
¶   extract from The Funeral Service within a Celebration of Holy Communion;
¶   General Rules;
¶   Supplementary Texts to Funeral;
¶   extracts from Resources for Funeral and Memorial Services;
¶   The Burial of Ashes.

For other material, page references to *Common Worship: Pastoral Services* are supplied.

Pagination   This booklet has two sets of page numbers. The outer numbers are the booklet's own page numbers, while the inner numbers near the centre of most pages refer to the equivalent pages in *Common Worship: Pastoral Services*.

Contents

Funeral

2   **The Outline Order for Funerals**

3   Pastoral Introduction

4   **The Funeral Service**

20   **The Funeral Service
within a Celebration of Holy Communion: Structure**

21   Notes to the Funeral Service

23   General Rules for Regulating Authorized Forms of Service

24   **Supplementary Texts**
Sentences 24
Some Texts which may be used by the Minister 26
The Blessing of a Grave 29

30   Bible Readings

39   Prayers of Entrusting and Commending

44   **The Burial of Ashes**

52   Psalms

66   Canticles

76   Authorization

77   Acknowledgements

In preparing for a Funeral, the minister should refer to the full provisions of the Funeral section in Common Worship: Pastoral Services *(pages 214–401).*

The Outline Order for Funerals

For Notes, see pages 21–22.

The Gathering

1 The coffin may be received at the door by the minister.
2 Sentences of Scripture may be used.
3 The minister welcomes the people and introduces the service.
4 A tribute or tributes may be made.
5 Authorized Prayers of Penitence may be used.
6 The Collect may be said here or in the Prayers.

Readings and Sermon

7 One or more readings from the Bible is used.
  Psalms or hymns may follow the readings.
8 A sermon is preached.

Prayers

9 The prayers usually follow this sequence:

¶ Thanksgiving for the life of the departed

¶ Prayer for those who mourn

¶ Prayers of Penitence (if not already used)

¶ Prayer for readiness to live in the light of eternity

Commendation and Farewell

10 The dead person is commended to God with authorized words.

The Committal

11 The body is committed to its resting place with authorized words.

The Dismissal

12 The service may end with a blessing.

If the Funeral Service takes place within a celebration of Holy Communion, the material on pages 282–290 in Common Worship: Pastoral Services *is followed for the Liturgy of the Sacrament (see also page 20 in this booklet).*

The Funeral

¶ *Pastoral Introduction*

This may be read by those present before the service begins.

God's love and power extend over all creation. Every life, including our own, is precious to God. Christians have always believed that there is hope in death as in life, and that there is new life in Christ over death.

Even those who share such faith find that there is a real sense of loss at the death of a loved one. We will each have had our own experiences of their life and death, with different memories and different feelings of love, grief and respect. To acknowledge this at the beginning of the service should help us to use this occasion to express our faith and our feelings as we say farewell, to acknowledge our loss and our sorrow, and to reflect on our own mortality. Those who mourn need support and consolation. Our presence here today is part of that continuing support.

The Funeral Service

Structure

¶ **The Gathering**
[Sentences]
Introduction
[Prayer]
[Prayers of Penitence]
The Collect

¶ **Readings and Sermon**

¶ **Prayers**

¶ **Commendation and Farewell**

¶ **The Committal**

¶ **The Dismissal**

For Notes, see pages 21–22.

The Funeral Service

¶ *The Gathering*

The coffin may be received by the minister (see Note 7 on page 22).
One or more sentences of Scripture may be used.

'I am the resurrection and the life,' says the Lord. 'Those who believe in me, even though they die, will live, and everyone who lives and believes in me will never die.'   *John 11.25,26*

I am convinced that neither death, nor life, nor angels, nor rulers, nor things present, nor things to come, nor powers, nor height, nor depth, nor anything else in all creation, will be able to separate us from the love of God in Christ Jesus our Lord.   *Romans 8.38,39*

Since we believe that Jesus died and rose again, even so, through Jesus, God will bring with him those who have died. So we will be with the Lord for ever. Therefore encourage one another with these words.   *1 Thessalonians 4.14,17b,18*

We brought nothing into the world, and we take nothing out. The Lord gave, and the Lord has taken away; blessed be the name of the Lord.   *1 Timothy 6.7; Job 1.21b*

The steadfast love of the Lord never ceases, his mercies never come to an end; they are new every morning; great is his faithfulness.
Lamentations 3.22,23

Blessed are those who mourn, for they will be comforted.
Matthew 5.4

God so loved the world that he gave his only Son, so that everyone who believes in him may not perish but may have eternal life.
John 3.16

Introduction

The minister says

We meet in the name of Jesus Christ,
who died and was raised to the glory of God the Father.
Grace and mercy be with you.

The minister introduces the service in these or other suitable words

We have come here today
to remember before God our *brother/sister N*;
to give thanks for *his/her* life;
to commend *him/her* to God our merciful redeemer and judge;
to commit *his/her* body to be *buried/cremated,*
and to comfort one another in our grief.

The minister may say one of these prayers

God of all consolation,
your Son Jesus Christ was moved to tears
at the grave of Lazarus his friend.
Look with compassion on your children in their loss;
give to troubled hearts the light of hope
and strengthen in us the gift of faith,
in Jesus Christ our Lord.

All **Amen.**

(or)

Almighty God,
you judge us with infinite mercy and justice
and love everything you have made.
In your mercy
turn the darkness of death into the dawn of new life,
and the sorrow of parting into the joy of heaven;
through our Saviour, Jesus Christ.

All **Amen.**

A hymn may be sung.
A brief tribute may be made (see Note 4 on page 21).

Prayers of Penitence

These or similar words may be used to introduce the confession

As children of a loving heavenly Father,
let us ask his forgiveness,
for he is gentle and full of compassion.

Silence may be kept.

These words may be used

God of mercy,
we acknowledge that we are all sinners.
We turn from the wrong that we have thought and said and done,
and are mindful of all that we have failed to do.
For the sake of Jesus, who died for us,
forgive us for all that is past,
and help us to live each day
in the light of Christ our Lord.

All **Amen.**

(or)

Lord, have mercy.
All **Lord, have mercy.**

Christ, have mercy.
All **Christ, have mercy.**

Lord, have mercy.
All **Lord, have mercy.**

The minister may say

May God our Father forgive us our sins
and bring us to the eternal joy of his kingdom,
where dust and ashes have no dominion.

All **Amen.**

The Collect

*The minister invites the people to pray, silence is kept and the
minister says this or another suitable Collect (see page 350 in
Common Worship: Pastoral Services)*

Merciful Father,
hear our prayers and comfort us;
renew our trust in your Son,
whom you raised from the dead;
strengthen our faith
that all who have died in the love of Christ
will share in his resurrection;
who lives and reigns with you,
in the unity of the Holy Spirit,
one God, now and for ever.

All   **Amen.**

*A reading from the Old or New Testament may be read
(see pages 30–38).*

This or another psalm or hymn is used (see Note 2 on page 21)

1   The Lord is my shepherd; ♦
    therefore can I lack nothing.

2   He makes me lie down in green pastures ♦
    and leads me beside still waters.

3   He shall refresh my soul ♦
    and guide me in the paths of righteousness for his name's sake.

4   Though I walk through the valley of the shadow of death,
        I will fear no evil; ♦
    for you are with me;
        your rod and your staff, they comfort me.

5   You spread a table before me
        in the presence of those who trouble me; ♦
    you have anointed my head with oil
        and my cup shall be full.

6   Surely goodness and loving mercy shall follow me
        all the days of my life, ♦
    and I will dwell in the house of the Lord for ever.   *Psalm 23*

*A reading from the New Testament (which may be a Gospel reading)
is used.*

A sermon is preached.

God of mercy, Lord of life,
you have made us in your image
to reflect your truth and light:
we give you thanks for *N*,
for the grace and mercy *he/she* received from you,
for all that was good in *his/her* life,
for the memories we treasure today.
[*Especially we thank you* …]
Silence
[Lord, in your mercy

All   **hear our prayer.**]

You promised eternal life to those who believe.
Remember for good this your servant *N*
as we also remember *him/her*.
Bring all who rest in Christ
into the fullness of your kingdom
where sins have been forgiven
and death is no more.
Silence
[Lord, in your mercy

All   **hear our prayer.**]

Your mighty power brings joy out of grief
and life out of death.
Look in mercy on [… *and*] all who mourn.
Give them patient faith in times of darkness.
Strengthen them with the knowledge of your love.

[Lord, in your mercy

All **hear our prayer.**]

You are tender towards your children
and your mercy is over all your works.
Heal the memories of hurt and failure.
Give us the wisdom and grace to use aright
the time that is left to us here on earth,
to turn to Christ and follow in his steps
in the way that leads to everlasting life.
Silence
[Lord, in your mercy

All **hear our prayer.**]

All **God of mercy,**
entrusting into your hands all that you have made
and rejoicing in our communion with all your
faithful people,
we make our prayers through Jesus Christ our Saviour.
Amen.

As our Saviour taught us, so we pray

All **Our Father in heaven,**
hallowed be your name,
your kingdom come,
your will be done,
on earth as in heaven.
Give us today our daily bread.
Forgive us our sins
as we forgive those who sin against us.
Lead us not into temptation
but deliver us from evil.
For the kingdom, the power,
and the glory are yours
now and for ever.
Amen.

(or)

Let us pray with confidence as our Saviour has taught us

All **Our Father, who art in heaven,**
hallowed be thy name;
thy kingdom come;
thy will be done;
on earth as it is in heaven.
Give us this day our daily bread.
And forgive us our trespasses,
as we forgive those who trespass against us.
And lead us not into temptation;
but deliver us from evil.
For thine is the kingdom,
the power and the glory,
for ever and ever.
Amen.

A hymn may be sung.

*The minister stands by the coffin and may invite others to gather
around it.*

The minister says

Let us commend N to the mercy of God,
our maker and redeemer.

Silence is kept.

*The minister uses this or another prayer of entrusting
and commending (see pages 39–43)*

God our creator and redeemer,
by your power Christ conquered death
and entered into glory.
Confident of his victory
and claiming his promises,
we entrust N to your mercy
in the name of Jesus our Lord,
who died and is alive
and reigns with you,
now and for ever.

All   **Amen.**

*If the Committal does not follow as part of the same service in the
same place, some sections of the Dismissal (pages 16–19) may be
used here.*

Sentences of Scripture may be used (pages 24–25).

The minister says

either

The Lord is full of compassion and mercy,
slow to anger and of great goodness.
As a father is tender towards his children,
so is the Lord tender to those that fear him.
For he knows of what we are made;
he remembers that we are but dust.
Our days are like the grass;
we flourish like a flower of the field;
when the wind goes over it, it is gone
and its place will know it no more.
But the merciful goodness of the Lord endures
        for ever and ever toward those that fear him
and his righteousness upon their children's children.

(or)

We have but a short time to live.
Like a flower we blossom and then wither;
like a shadow we flee and never stay.
In the midst of life we are in death;
to whom can we turn for help,
but to you, Lord, who are justly angered by our sins?
Yet, Lord God most holy, Lord most mighty,
O holy and most merciful Saviour,
deliver us from the bitter pain of eternal death.
Lord, you know the secrets of our hearts;
hear our prayer, O God most mighty;
spare us, most worthy judge eternal;
at our last hour let us not fall from you,
O holy and merciful Saviour.

We have entrusted our *brother/sister* N to God's mercy,
and we now commit *his/her* body to the ground:
earth to earth, ashes to ashes, dust to dust:
in sure and certain hope of the resurrection to eternal life
through our Lord Jesus Christ,
who will transform our frail bodies
that they may be conformed to his glorious body,
who died, was buried, and rose again for us.
To him be glory for ever.

All **Amen.**

(or)

in a crematorium, if the Committal is to follow at the Burial of the Ashes

We have entrusted our *brother/sister* N to God's mercy,
and now, in preparation for burial,
we give *his/her* body to be cremated.
We look for the fullness of the resurrection
when Christ shall gather all his saints
to reign with him in glory for ever.

All **Amen.**

(or)

in a crematorium, if the Committal is to take place then

We have entrusted our *brother/sister* N to God's mercy,
and we now commit *his/her* body to be cremated:
earth to earth, ashes to ashes, dust to dust:
in sure and certain hope of the resurrection to eternal life
through our Lord Jesus Christ,
who will transform our frail bodies
that they may be conformed to his glorious body,
who died, was buried, and rose again for us.
To him be glory for ever.

All **Amen.**

The Lord's Prayer

As our Saviour taught us, so we pray

All   **Our Father in heaven,**
hallowed be your name,
your kingdom come,
your will be done,
on earth as in heaven.
Give us today our daily bread.
Forgive us our sins
as we forgive those who sin against us.
Lead us not into temptation
but deliver us from evil.
For the kingdom, the power,
and the glory are yours
now and for ever.
Amen.

(or)

Let us pray with confidence as our Saviour has taught us

All   **Our Father, who art in heaven,**
hallowed be thy name;
thy kingdom come;
thy will be done;
on earth as it is in heaven.
Give us this day our daily bread.
And forgive us our trespasses,
as we forgive those who trespass against us.
And lead us not into temptation;
but deliver us from evil.
For thine is the kingdom,
the power and the glory,
for ever and ever.
Amen.

Nunc dimittis (The Song of Simeon)

1   Now, Lord, you let your servant go in peace: ◆
your word has been fulfilled.

2   My own eyes have seen the salvation ◆
which you have prepared in the sight of every people;

3   A light to reveal you to the nations ◆
and the glory of your people Israel.   *Luke 2.29-32*

Glory to the Father and to the Son
and to the Holy Spirit;
as it was in the beginning is now
and shall be for ever. Amen.

Prayers

One or more of these prayers, or other suitable prayers, may be used

All   **Heavenly Father,**
in your Son Jesus Christ
you have given us a true faith and a sure hope.
Strengthen this faith and hope in us all our days,
that we may live as those who believe in
    the communion of saints,
    the forgiveness of sins
    and the resurrection to eternal life;
through Jesus Christ our Lord.
Amen.

All   **God be in my head,**
and in my understanding;
God be in my eyes,
and in my looking;
God be in my mouth,
and in my speaking;
God be in my heart,
and in my thinking;
God be at my end,
and at my departing.
Amen.

Support us, O Lord,
all the day long of this troublous life,
until the shadows lengthen and the evening comes,
the busy world is hushed,
the fever of life is over
and our work is done.
Then, Lord, in your mercy grant us a safe lodging,
a holy rest, and peace at the last;
through Christ our Lord.

All **Amen.**

Ending

One of these, or another suitable ending, may be used

May God in his infinite love and mercy
bring the whole Church,
living and departed in the Lord Jesus,
to a joyful resurrection
and the fulfilment of his eternal kingdom.

All **Amen.**

May God give *you*
his comfort and his peace,
his light and his joy,
in this world and the next;
and the blessing of God almighty,
the Father, the Son, and the Holy Spirit,
be among *you* and remain with *you* always.

All **Amen.**

God will show us the path of life;
in his presence is the fullness of joy:
and at his right hand
there is pleasure for evermore.

cf Psalm 16.11

Unto him that is able to keep us from falling,
and to present us faultless before the presence of his glory
    with exceeding joy,
to the only wise God our Saviour,
be glory and majesty,
dominion and power,
both now and ever.
All **Amen.**   *Jude 24,25*

The Funeral Service within a Celebration of Holy Communion

Structure

¶ **The Gathering**
[Sentences]
[Introduction]
[Prayer]
Prayers of Penitence
The Collect

¶ **The Liturgy of the Word**
Reading(s)
Gospel Reading
Sermon

¶ **Prayers**

¶ **The Liturgy of the Sacrament**
The Peace
Preparation of the Table
Taking of the Bread and Wine
The Eucharistic Prayer
The Lord's Prayer
Breaking of the Bread
Giving of Communion
Prayer after Communion

¶ **Commendation and Farewell**

¶ **The Committal**

¶ **The Dismissal**

For Notes, see pages 21–22.

For a full text of the Funeral Service within a Celebration of Holy Communion, see pages 275–290 in Common Worship: Pastoral Services.

Notes to the Funeral Service

1   Sentences

Sentences of Scripture may be used at the entry, after the
Introduction, or at other suitable points.

2   Psalms and Readings

Psalms and Readings should normally be drawn from those set out
on pages 30–38 and 52–65. A psalm should normally be used. It may
be in a metrical or hymn version, or be replaced by a scriptural song
(for Canticles, see pages 66–74). There must always be one reading
from the Bible.

3   Hymns

Points are suggested for these, but they may be sung at any
suitable point.

4   Tribute

Remembering and honouring the life of the person who has died,
and the evidence of God's grace and work in them, should be done
in the earlier part of the service, after the opening prayer, though
if occasion demands it may be woven into the sermon or come
immediately before the Commendation. It may be done in
conjunction with the placing of symbols, and may be spoken by
a family member or friend or by the minister using information
provided by the family. It is preferable not to interrupt the flow
of the Reading(s) and sermon with a tribute of this kind.

5   Sermon

The purpose of the sermon is to proclaim the gospel in the context
of the death of this particular person.

6   Creed

An authorized Creed or an authorized Affirmation of Faith may be
said after the sermon.

For Notes 7–9, see over.

7 Receiving the coffin

The coffin may be received into the church at the beginning of the service, or earlier in the day, or on the day before the funeral.

¶ A candle may stand beside the coffin and may be carried in front of the coffin when it is brought into the church.

¶ The coffin may be sprinkled with water on entry. This may occur at the Commendation, or at the Committal.

¶ A pall may be placed over the coffin in church by family, friends or other members of the congregation.

¶ Before or at the start of the service or after the opening prayer and hymn, and with the minister's agreement, suitable symbols of the life and faith of the departed person may be placed on or near the coffin.

¶ At the sprinkling, the placing of the pall or symbols, the words on pages 26–27 may be used.

8 The Committal

The Committal is used at the point at which it is needed, for example:

¶ at the burial of the body in a cemetery or churchyard,

¶ at the interment of ashes when this follows on the same day or the day following cremation, in which case the second 'preparation for burial' prayer (page 15) is used at the crematorium, or

¶ at a crematorium when the interment of ashes is not to follow immediately.

Forms of Commendation and Committal are provided, but when occasion demands, other authorized forms may be used.

When the body or the ashes are to be deposited in a vault, mausoleum or brick grave, these words may be used at the committal:

We have entrusted our *brother/sister N* to God's mercy, and now we commit *his/her* body to its resting place.

9 The Funeral Service within Holy Communion

The Notes to the Order for the Celebration of Holy Communion, as well as the Notes to the Funeral Service, apply equally to this service. Texts are suggested at different points, but other suitable texts may be used. In the Liturgy of the Word, there should be a Gospel reading, preceded by either one or two other readings from the Bible.

General Rules for Regulating Authorized Forms of Service

1. Any reference in authorized provision to the use of hymns shall be construed as including the use of texts described as songs, chants, canticles.

2. If occasion requires, hymns may be sung at points other than those indicated in particular forms of service. Silence may be kept at points other than those indicated in particular forms of service.

3. Where rubrics indicate that a text is to be 'said' this must be understood to include 'or sung' and vice versa.

4. Where parts of a service make use of well-known and traditional texts, other translations or versions, particularly when used in musical compositions, may be used.

5. Local custom may be established and followed in respect of posture but regard should be had to indications in Notes attached to authorized forms of service that a particular posture is appropriate for some parts of that form of service.

6. On any occasion when the text of an alternative service authorized under the provisions of Canon B 2 provides for the Lord's Prayer to be said or sung, it may be used in the form included in *The Book of Common Prayer* or in either of the two other forms included in services in *Common Worship*. The further text included in Prayers for Various Occasions (page 106 in *Common Worship: Services and Prayers for the Church of England*) may be used on suitable occasions.

7. Normally on any occasion only one Collect is used.

8. At Baptisms, Confirmations, Ordinations and Marriages which take place on Principal Feasts, other Principal Holy Days and on Sundays of Advent, Lent and Easter, within the Celebration of the Holy Communion, the Readings of the day are used and the Collect of the Day is said, unless the bishop directs otherwise.

9. The Collects and Lectionary in *Common Worship* may, optionally, be used in conjunction with the days included in the Calendar of *The Book of Common Prayer*, notwithstanding any difference in the title or name of a Sunday, Holy Day or other observance included in both Calendars.

Supplementary Texts

God will show us the path of life; in his presence is the fullness of joy: at his right hand there is pleasure for evermore.   *cf Psalm 16.10*

God is our refuge and strength, a very present help in trouble.
Psalm 46.1

Out of the depths have I cried to you, O Lord; Lord, hear my voice; let your ears consider well the voice of my supplications.
cf Psalm 130.1

I know that my Redeemer lives, and that at the last he will stand upon the earth; and after my skin has been destroyed, then in my flesh I shall see God, whom I shall see for myself, and my eyes shall behold, and not another.   *Job 19.25-27*

As they came from their mother's womb, so they shall go again, naked as they came; they shall take nothing for their toil, which they may carry away with their hands. This also is a grievous ill: just as they came, so shall they go; and what gain do they have from toiling for the wind?   *Ecclesiastes 5.15,16*

The steadfast love of the Lord never ceases, his mercies never come to an end; they are new every morning; great is his faithfulness.
Lamentations 3.22,23

Blessed are those who mourn, for they will be comforted.
Matthew 5.4

The king will say to those at his right hand, 'Come, you that are blessed by my Father, inherit the kingdom prepared for you from the foundation of the world.'   *Matthew 25.34*

Jesus said, 'Truly I tell you, today you will be with me in Paradise.'
Luke 23.43

God so loved the world that he gave his only Son, so that everyone who believes in him may not perish but may have eternal life.
John 3.16

This is indeed the will of my Father, that all who see the Son and believe in him may have eternal life; and I will raise them up on the last day.   *John 6.40*

'I am the resurrection and the life,' says the Lord. 'Those who
believe in me, even though they die, will live, and everyone who
lives and believes in me will never die.'   *John 11.25,26*

In my Father's house there are many dwelling places. If it were not
so, would I have told you that I go to prepare a place for you? And if
I go and prepare a place for you, I will come again and will take you
to myself, so that where I am, there you may be also.   *John 14.2,3*

I am convinced that neither death, nor life, nor angels, nor rulers,
nor things present, nor things to come, nor powers, nor height,
nor depth, nor anything else in all creation, will be able to separate
us from the love of God in Christ Jesus our Lord.   *Romans 8.38,39*

What no eye has seen, nor ear heard, nor the human heart
conceived, what God has prepared for those who love him – these
things God has revealed to us through the Spirit.
                                                    1 Corinthians 2.9-10a

He must reign until he has put all his enemies under his feet.
The last enemy to be destroyed is death.   *1 Corinthians 15.25,26*

Blessed be the God and Father of our Lord Jesus Christ, the Father
of mercies and God of all comfort, who comforts us in all our
affliction, so that we may be able to comfort those who are in any
affliction, with the comfort with which we ourselves are comforted
by God.   *2 Corinthians 1.3,4*

We know that if the earthly tent we live in is destroyed, we have a
building from God, a house not made with hands, eternal in the
heavens.   *2 Corinthians 5.1*

We believe that Jesus died and rose again; and so it will be for those
who died as Christians; God will bring them to life with Jesus.
Thus we shall always be with the Lord. Comfort one another with
these words.   *cf 1 Thessalonians 4.14,17b,18*

We brought nothing into the world, and we take nothing out.
The Lord gave, and the Lord has taken away; blessed be the name
of the Lord.   *1 Timothy 6.7; Job 1.21b*

At the Celebration of Holy Communion

Jesus said, 'Whoever eats my flesh and drinks my blood has eternal
life, and I will raise him up on the last day.' [Alleluia.]   *John 6.54*

Note

The coffin may be received into the church at the beginning of the Funeral Service, or earlier in the day, or on the day before the Funeral. A candle may stand beside the coffin and may be carried in front of the coffin when it is brought into the church.

Receiving the coffin

We receive the body of our *brother/sister N*
with confidence in God, the giver of life,
who raised the Lord Jesus from the dead.

Sprinkling the coffin with water

With this water we call to mind *N*'s baptism.
As Christ went through the deep waters of death for us,
so may he bring us to the fullness of resurrection life
with *N* and all the redeemed.

(or)

Grant, Lord,
that we who are baptized into the death
    of your Son our Saviour Jesus Christ
may continually put to death our evil desires
    and be buried with him;
and that through the grave and gate of death
we may pass to our joyful resurrection;
through his merits,
who died and was buried and rose again for us,
your Son Jesus Christ our Lord.

All   **Amen.**

Suitable sentences of Scripture may be used (see pages 24–25).

God our Father,
by raising Christ your Son you destroyed the power of death
and opened for us the way to eternal life.
As we remember before you our *brother/sister N,*
we ask your help for all who shall gather in *his/her* memory.
Grant us the assurance of your presence and grace,
by the Spirit you have given us;
through Jesus Christ our Lord.

All   **Amen.**

Covering the coffin with a pall

We are already God's children,
but what we shall be has not yet been revealed.
Yet we know that when Christ appears we shall be like him,
for we shall see him as he is.

(or)

On Mount Zion the Lord will remove the pall of sorrow
hanging over all nations.
He will destroy death for ever.
He will wipe away the tears from every face.

Placing a Bible on the coffin

Lord Jesus Christ,
your living and imperishable word brings us to new birth.
Your eternal promises to us and to *N* are proclaimed in the Bible.

Placing a cross on the coffin

Lord Jesus Christ,
for love of *N* and each one of us
you bore our sins on the cross.

*With the minister's agreement, other suitable symbols of the life and
faith of the departed person may be placed on or near the coffin.
Those present may be encouraged to share briefly their memories
of the one who has died.*

Heavenly Father,
you have not made us for darkness and death,
but for life with you for ever.
Without you we have nothing to hope for;
with you we have nothing to fear.
Speak to us now your words of eternal life.
Lift us from anxiety and guilt
to the light and peace of your presence,
and set the glory of your love before us;
through Jesus Christ our Lord.

All   **Amen.**

*John 14.1-6 or other appropriate readings may be read, with psalms
and prayers and silence (see pages 30–38 and 52–65 in this booklet
and 345–382 in* Common Worship: Pastoral Services*).*

Almighty God,
you love everything you have made
and judge us with infinite mercy and justice.
We rejoice in your promises of pardon, joy and peace
to all those who love you.
In your mercy turn the darkness of death into the dawn of new life
and the sorrow of parting into the joy of heaven;
through our Saviour Jesus Christ,
who died, who rose again, and lives for evermore.

All   **Amen.**

*The minister uses one or more of these prayers. The service
may end with a time of silence. As they leave, the mourners may
come near and touch the coffin, or gather round it and pray.*

N has fallen asleep in the peace of Christ.
As we leave *his/her* body here, we entrust *him/her*,
with faith and hope in everlasting life,
to the love and mercy of our Father
and surround *him/her* with our love and prayer.
[In baptism, *he/she* was made by adoption a child of God.
At the eucharist *he/she* was sustained and fed.
God now welcomes *him/her* to his table in heaven
to share in eternal life with all the saints.]

God of all consolation,
your Son Jesus Christ was moved to tears
at the grave of Lazarus his friend.
Look with compassion on your children in their loss;
give to troubled hearts the light of hope
and strengthen in us the gift of faith,
in Jesus Christ our Lord.

All **Amen.**

The Lord God almighty is our Father:

All **he loves us and tenderly cares for us.**

The Lord Jesus Christ is our Saviour:

All **he has redeemed us and will defend us to the end.**

The Lord, the Holy Spirit is among us:

All **he will lead us in God's holy way.**

To God almighty, Father, Son, and Holy Spirit,

All **be praise and glory today and for ever. Amen.**

¶ *The Blessing of a Grave*

O God,
whose Son Jesus Christ was laid in a tomb:
bless, we pray, this grave
as the place where the body of *N* your servant
    may rest in peace,
through your Son, who is the resurrection and the life;
who died and is alive and reigns with you
now and for ever.

All **Amen.**

Bible Readings

Any suitable translation may be used.

For further Readings, see pages 37–38.
For Psalms and Canticles, see pages 52–75.

John 6.35-40

Jesus said to them, 'I am the bread of life. Whoever comes to me will never be hungry, and whoever believes in me will never be thirsty. But I said to you that you have seen me and yet do not believe. Everything that the Father gives me will come to me, and anyone who comes to me I will never drive away; for I have come down from heaven, not to do my own will, but the will of him who sent me. And this is the will of him who sent me, that I should lose nothing of all that he has given me, but raise it up on the last day. This is indeed the will of my Father, that all who see the Son and believe in him may have eternal life; and I will raise them up on the last day.'

John 11.17-27

When Jesus arrived, he found that Lazarus had already been in the tomb for four days. Now Bethany was near Jerusalem, some two miles away, and many of the Jews had come to Martha and Mary to console them about their brother. When Martha heard that Jesus was coming, she went and met him, while Mary stayed at home. Martha said to Jesus, 'Lord, if you had been here, my brother would not have died. But even now I know that God will give you whatever you ask of him.' Jesus said to her, 'Your brother will rise again.' Martha said to him, 'I know that he will rise again in the resurrection on the last day.' Jesus said to her, 'I am the resurrection and the life. Those who believe in me, even though they die, will live, and everyone who lives and believes in me will never die. Do you believe this?' She said to him, 'Yes, Lord, I believe that you are the Messiah, the Son of God, the one coming into the world.'

Jesus said to his disciples: 'Do not let your hearts be troubled. Believe in God, believe also in me. In my Father's house there are many dwelling places. If it were not so, would I have told you that I go to prepare a place for you? And if I go and prepare a place for you, I will come again and will take you to myself, so that where I am, there you may be also. And you know the way to the place where I am going.' Thomas said to him, 'Lord, we do not know where you are going. How can we know the way?' Jesus said to him, 'I am the way, and the truth, and the life. No one comes to the Father except through me.'

Romans 8.31-end

What then are we to say about these things? If God is for us, who is against us? He who did not withhold his own Son, but gave him up for all of us, will he not with him also give us everything else? Who will bring any charge against God's elect? It is God who justifies. Who is to condemn? It is Christ Jesus, who died, yes, who was raised, who is at the right hand of God, who indeed intercedes for us. Who will separate us from the love of Christ? Will hardship, or distress, or persecution, or famine, or nakedness, or peril, or sword? As it is written,

'For your sake we are being killed all day long;
we are accounted as sheep to be slaughtered.'

No, in all these things we are more than conquerors through him who loved us. For I am convinced that neither death, nor life, nor angels, nor rulers, nor things present, nor things to come, nor powers, nor height, nor depth, nor anything else in all creation, will be able to separate us from the love of God in Christ Jesus our Lord.

I should remind you, brothers and sisters, of the good news that
I proclaimed to you, which you in turn received, in which also you
stand, through which also you are being saved, if you hold firmly
to the message that I proclaimed to you – unless you have come
to believe in vain.

For I handed on to you as of first importance what I in turn had
received: that Christ died for our sins in accordance with the
scriptures, and that he was buried, and that he was raised on the
third day in accordance with the scriptures, and that he appeared
to Cephas, then to the twelve. Then he appeared to more than five
hundred brothers and sisters at one time, most of whom are still
alive, though some have died. Then he appeared to James, then to
all the apostles. Last of all, as to one untimely born, he appeared
also to me. For I am the least of the apostles, unfit to be called an
apostle, because I persecuted the church of God. But by the grace
of God I am what I am, and his grace towards me has not been in
vain. On the contrary, I worked harder than any of them – though
it was not I, but the grace of God that is with me. Whether then it
was I or they, so we proclaim and so you have come to believe.

Now if Christ is proclaimed as raised from the dead, how can
some of you say there is no resurrection of the dead? If there is
no resurrection of the dead, then Christ has not been raised; and
if Christ has not been raised, then our proclamation has been in
vain and your faith has been in vain. We are even found to be
misrepresenting God, because we testified of God that he raised
Christ – whom he did not raise if it is true that the dead are not
raised. For if the dead are not raised, then Christ has not been
raised. If Christ has not been raised, your faith is futile and you
are still in your sins. Then those also who have died in Christ have
perished. If for this life only we have hoped in Christ, we are of all
people most to be pitied.

But in fact Christ has been raised from the dead, the first fruits of
those who have died. For since death came through a human being,
the resurrection of the dead has also come through a human being;
for as all die in Adam, so all will be made alive in Christ. But each in
his own order: Christ the first fruits, then at his coming those who
belong to Christ. Then comes the end, when he hands over the

kingdom to God the Father, after he has destroyed every ruler and
every authority and power. For he must reign until he has put all
his enemies under his feet. The last enemy to be destroyed is death.

But someone will ask, 'How are the dead raised? With what kind
of body do they come?' Fool! What you sow does not come to life
unless it dies. And as for what you sow, you do not sow the body
that is to be, but a bare seed, perhaps of wheat or of some other
grain. But God gives it a body as he has chosen, and to each kind
of seed its own body.

So it is with the resurrection of the dead. What is sown is
perishable, what is raised is imperishable. It is sown in dishonour,
it is raised in glory. It is sown in weakness, it is raised in power.
It is sown a physical body, it is raised a spiritual body.

For this perishable body must put on imperishability, and this
mortal body must put on immortality. When this perishable body
puts on imperishability, and this mortal body puts on immortality,
then the saying that is written will be fulfilled:

'Death has been swallowed up in victory.'
'Where, O death, is your victory?
Where, O death, is your sting?'

The sting of death is sin, and the power of sin is the law. But thanks
be to God, who gives us the victory through our Lord Jesus Christ.

Therefore, my beloved, be steadfast, immovable, always excelling
in the work of the Lord, because you know that in the Lord your
labour is not in vain.

But in fact Christ has been raised from the dead, the first fruits of those who have died. For since death came through a human being, the resurrection of the dead has also come through a human being; for as all die in Adam, so all will be made alive in Christ. But each in his own order: Christ the first fruits, then at his coming those who belong to Christ. Then comes the end, when he hands over the kingdom to God the Father, after he has destroyed every ruler and every authority and power. For he must reign until he has put all his enemies under his feet. The last enemy to be destroyed is death. For 'God has put all things in subjection under his feet.' But when it says, 'All things are put in subjection,' it is plain that this does not include the one who put all things in subjection under him. When all things are subjected to him, then the Son himself will also be subjected to the one who put all things in subjection under him, so that God may be all in all.

Otherwise, what will those people do who receive baptism on behalf of the dead? If the dead are not raised at all, why are people baptized on their behalf?

And why are we putting ourselves in danger every hour? I die every day! That is as certain, brothers and sisters, as my boasting of you – a boast that I make in Christ Jesus our Lord. If with merely human hopes I fought with wild animals at Ephesus, what would I have gained by it? If the dead are not raised,

'Let us eat and drink,
for tomorrow we die.'

Do not be deceived:

'Bad company ruins good morals.'

Come to a sober and right mind, and sin no more; for some people have no knowledge of God. I say this to your shame.

But someone will ask, 'How are the dead raised? With what kind of body do they come?' Fool! What you sow does not come to life unless it dies. And as for what you sow, you do not sow the body that is to be, but a bare seed, perhaps of wheat or of some other grain. But God gives it a body as he has chosen, and to each kind of seed its own body. Not all flesh is alike, but there is one flesh for human beings, another for animals, another for birds, and another for fish. There are both heavenly bodies and earthly bodies, but the glory of the heavenly is one thing, and that of the earthly is another. There is one glory of the sun, and another glory of the moon, and another glory of the stars; indeed, star differs from star in glory.

So it is with the resurrection of the dead. What is sown is perishable, what is raised is imperishable. It is sown in dishonour, it is raised in glory. It is sown in weakness, it is raised in power. It is sown a physical body, it is raised a spiritual body. If there is a physical body, there is also a spiritual body. Thus it is written, 'The first man, Adam, became a living being'; the last Adam became a life-giving spirit. But it is not the spiritual that is first, but the physical, and then the spiritual. The first man was from the earth, a man of dust; the second man is from heaven. As was the man of dust, so are those who are of the dust; and as is the man of heaven, so are those who are of heaven. Just as we have borne the image of the man of dust, we will also bear the image of the man of heaven.

What I am saying, brothers and sisters, is this: flesh and blood cannot inherit the kingdom of God, nor does the perishable inherit the imperishable. Listen, I will tell you a mystery! We will not all die, but we will all be changed, in a moment, in the twinkling of an eye, at the last trumpet. For the trumpet will sound, and the dead will be raised imperishable, and we will be changed. For this perishable body must put on imperishability, and this mortal body must put on immortality. When this perishable body puts on imperishability, and this mortal body puts on immortality, then the saying that is written will be fulfilled:

'Death has been swallowed up in victory.'
'Where, O death, is your victory?
Where, O death, is your sting?'

The sting of death is sin, and the power of sin is the law. But thanks be to God, who gives us the victory through our Lord Jesus Christ.

Therefore, my beloved, be steadfast, immovable, always excelling in the work of the Lord, because you know that in the Lord your labour is not in vain.

We do not want you to be uninformed, brothers and sisters, about those who have died, so that you may not grieve as others do who have no hope. For since we believe that Jesus died and rose again, even so, through Jesus, God will bring with him those who have died. For this we declare to you by the word of the Lord, that we who are alive, who are left until the coming of the Lord, will by no means precede those who have died. For the Lord himself, with a cry of command, with the archangel's call and with the sound of God's trumpet, will descend from heaven, and the dead in Christ will rise first. Then we who are alive, who are left, will be caught up in the clouds together with them to meet the Lord in the air; and so we will be with the Lord for ever. Therefore encourage one another with these words.

Revelation 21.1-7

I, John, saw a new heaven and a new earth; for the first heaven and the first earth had passed away, and the sea was no more. And I saw the holy city, the new Jerusalem, coming down out of heaven from God, prepared as a bride adorned for her husband. And I heard a loud voice from the throne saying,

'See, the home of God is among mortals.
He will dwell with them;
they will be his peoples,
and God himself will be with them;
he will wipe every tear from their eyes.
Death will be no more;
mourning and crying and pain will be no more,
for the first things have passed away.'

And the one who was seated on the throne said, 'See, I am making all things new.' Also he said, 'Write this, for these words are trustworthy and true.' Then he said to me, 'It is done! I am the Alpha and the Omega, the beginning and the end. To the thirsty I will give water as a gift from the spring of the water of life. Those who conquer will inherit these things, and I will be their God and they will be my children.'

Old Testament and Apocrypha

Genesis 42.29-end *The sorrow you would cause me would kill me*
2 Samuel 1.17,23-end *David's lament for Saul and Jonathan*
2 Samuel 12.16-23 *David's son dies*
Job 19.23-27 *I know that my Redeemer lives*
Isaiah 53.1-10 *The suffering servant*
Isaiah 61.1-3 *To comfort all who mourn*
Lamentations 3.22-26,31-33 *The love of the Lord never ceases*
Daniel 12.1-3[5-9] *Everyone whose name shall be found written
    in the book*
Wisdom 2.22 – 3.5,9 *The souls of the righteous are in the hand of God*
Wisdom 3.1-5,9 *The souls of the righteous are in the hand of God*
Wisdom 4.8-11,13-15 *Age is not length of time*
Ecclesiasticus 38.16-23 *Do not forget, there is no coming back*

Psalms

See pages 52–65.

Psalm 6	Psalm 32	Psalm 116
Psalm 23	Psalm 38.9-end	Psalm 118.4-end
Psalm 25	Psalm 42	Psalm 121
Psalm 27	Psalm 90	Psalm 139

New Testament

The passages printed on pages 30–36 are included in this list.

Matthew 25.31-end *The final judgement*
Mark 10.13-16 *Let the little children come to me*
Mark 15.33-39; 16.1-6 *He has risen, he is not here*
Luke 12.35-40 *The coming of the Son of Man*
Luke 24.1-9[10-11] *The Resurrection*
John 5.[19-20]21-29 *Whoever hears my word and believes him who
    sent me, has eternal life*

John 6.35-40[53-58] *All that the Father gives me will come to me*
John 11.17-27 *I am the resurrection and the life*
John 14.1-6 *In my Father's house are many rooms*
John 19.38-end *The burial of Christ*
John 20.1-11 *The Resurrection of Christ*
Romans 6.3-8[9-11] *All of us who have been baptized into
Christ Jesus were baptized into his death*
Romans 8.18-25[26-30] *The future glory*
Romans 8.31-end *Nothing can separate us from the love of Christ*
Romans 14.7-12 *Christ the Lord of the living and the dead*
1 Corinthians 15.1-26,35-38,42-44a,53-end *The resurrection of the dead*
1 Corinthians 15.20-end *The resurrection of the dead*
2 Corinthians 4.7-15 *We carry in our mortal bodies the death of Jesus*
2 Corinthians 4.16 – 5.10 *The heavenly body*
Ephesians 3.14-19[20-21] *The power to understand Christ's love*
Philippians 3.10-end *God's purposes for us*
1 Thessalonians 4.13-18 *So we shall always be with the Lord*
2 Timothy 2.8-13 *If we have died with him, we shall also live with him*
1 Peter 1.3-9 *We have been born anew to a living hope*
1 John 3.1-3 *We shall be like him*
Revelation 7.9-end *The crowd worshipping in heaven*
Revelation 21.1-7 *Behold I make all things new*
Revelation 21.22-end; 22.3b-5 *The Lord God will be their light*

Psalm 84.1-4
Song of Solomon 2.10-13
Isaiah 49.15-16
Jeremiah 1.4-8
Jeremiah 31.15-17
Matthew 18.1-5,10
John 10.27,28
1 Corinthians 13.1-end

Prayers of Entrusting and Commending

These prayers are taken from Prayers for Use with the Dying and at Funeral and Memorial Services in Common Worship: Pastoral Services pages 346–382.

68   Lord Jesus, our redeemer,
you willingly gave yourself up to death,
so that all might be saved and pass from death to life.
By dying you unlocked the gates of life
for all those who believe in you.
So we commend *N* into your arms of mercy,
believing that, with sins forgiven,
he/she will share a place of happiness, light and peace
in the kingdom of your glory for ever.

All   **Amen.**

69   *N* has fallen asleep in the peace of Christ.
We entrust *him/her*, with faith and hope in everlasting life,
to the love and mercy of our Father
and surround *him/her* with our love and prayer.
[In baptism, *he/she* was made by adoption a child of God.
At the eucharist *he/she* was sustained and fed.
God now welcomes *him/her* to his table in heaven
to share in eternal life with all the saints.]

All   **Amen.**

70   Heavenly Father,
your Son Jesus Christ is the firstborn from the dead.
We believe that he will raise up the bodies of his faithful people
    to be like his in glory.
We commend *N* to your mercy
and pray that as you gather *him/her* to yourself,
you will give to us your blessing of peace;
through Jesus Christ our Lord,
who died and rose again to save us,
and is now alive and reigns with you
and the Holy Spirit in glory for ever.

All   **Amen.**

71 Heavenly Father,
    you have assured us
    that everyone who looks to your Son
    and believes in him
    shall have eternal life.
    Trusting in your faithfulness,
    we commend *N* to your mercy
    as we await that great day
    when you raise us with *him/her* to life in triumph
    and we shall stand before you,
    with all your whole creation made new in him,
    in the glory of your heavenly kingdom.
All **Amen.**

72 God our creator and redeemer,
    by your power Christ conquered death
    and returned to you in glory,
    bearing in his body the marks of his passion.
    Confident of your victory
    and claiming his promises,
    we entrust *N* into your keeping
    in the name of Jesus our Lord,
    who, though he died, is now alive
    and reigns with you and the Holy Spirit,
    one God, now and for ever.
All **Amen.**

73 Almighty God,
    as you bring us face to face with our mortality,
    we thank you for making each one of us in your own image
    and giving us gifts in body, mind and spirit.
    We thank you now as we honour the memory of *N*,
    whom you gave to us and have taken away.
    We entrust *him/her* to your mercy,
    and pray that you will show us the path of life,
    and the fullness of joy in your presence
    through all eternity.
All **Amen.**

74   Almighty God,
      in your great love
      you crafted us by your hand
      and breathed life into us by your Spirit.
      Although we became a rebellious people,
      you did not abandon us to our sin.
      In your tender mercy
      you sent your Son
      to restore in us your image.
      In obedience to your will
      he gave up his life for us,
      bearing in his body our sins on the cross.
      By your mighty power
      you raised him from the grave
      and exalted him to the throne of glory.
      Rejoicing in his victory
      and trusting in your promise
      to make alive all who turn to Christ,
      we commend *N* to your mercy
      and we join with all your faithful people
      and the whole company of heaven
      in the one unending song of praise:
      glory and wisdom and honour
      be to our God for ever and ever.

All   **Amen.**

At the time of death

75   Into your hands, Lord,
      our faithful creator and most loving redeemer,
      we commend your child *N*,
      for *he/she* is yours in death as in life.
      In your great mercy
      fulfil in *him/her* the purpose of your love;
      gather *him/her* to yourself in gentleness and peace,
      that, rejoicing in the light and refreshment of your presence,
      he/she may enjoy that rest which you have prepared
            for your faithful servants;
      through Jesus Christ our Lord.

All   **Amen.**

76   Into your hands, O merciful Saviour,
      we commend your servant N.
      Acknowledge, we pray, a sheep of your own fold,
      a lamb of your own flock,
      a sinner of your own redeeming.
      Enfold *him/her* in the arms of your mercy,
      in the blessed rest of everlasting peace
      and in the glorious company of the saints in light.
All **Amen.**

77   N, go forth from this world:
      in the love of God the Father who created you,
      in the mercy of Jesus Christ who redeemed you,
      in the power of the Holy Spirit who strengthens you.
      May the heavenly host sustain you
      and the company of heaven enfold you.
      In communion with all the faithful,
      may you dwell this day in peace.
All **Amen.**

78   N, go forth upon your journey from this world,
      in the name of God the Father almighty who created you;
      in the name of Jesus Christ who suffered death for you;
      in the name of the Holy Spirit who strengthens you;
      in communion with the blessed saints,
      and aided by angels and archangels,
      and all the armies of the heavenly host.
      May your portion this day be in peace,
      and your dwelling the heavenly Jerusalem.
All **Amen.**

All **Give rest, O Christ, to your servant with the saints:
where sorrow and pain are no more,
neither sighing, but life everlasting.**
You only are immortal, the creator and maker of all:
and we are mortal, formed from the dust of the earth,
and unto earth shall we return.
For so you ordained when you created me, saying:
'Dust you are and to dust you shall return.'
All of us go down to the dust,
yet weeping at the grave, we make our song:
Alleluia, alleluia, alleluia.

All **Give rest, O Christ, to your servant with the saints:
where sorrow and pain are no more,
neither sighing, but life everlasting.**

The Burial of Ashes

Note

If the service begins in church or chapel, it may be appropriate to
invite the mourners to the place of burial at the end of the readings,
and to use the psalms at the place of burial.

44

Preparation

The minister greets the people in these or other suitable words

Grace, mercy and peace
from God our Father and the Lord Jesus Christ
be with you all.

Though we are dust and ashes,
God has prepared for those who love him
    a heavenly dwelling place.
At *his/her* funeral we commended *N* into the hands
    of almighty God.
As we prepare to commit the remains of *N* to the earth,
we entrust ourselves and all who love God to his loving care.

Appropriate sentences of Scripture may be used.

The eternal God is our refuge,
and underneath are the everlasting arms.   *cf Deuteronomy 33. 27 AV*

Blessed be the God and Father of our Lord Jesus Christ!
By his great mercy he has given us a new birth into a living hope
    through the resurrection of Jesus Christ from the dead,
and into an inheritance that is imperishable, undefiled, and unfading,
kept in heaven for you.   *1 Peter 1.3,4*

Lord, you have been our refuge
from one generation to another.

Before the mountains were brought forth,
    or the earth and the world were formed,
from everlasting to everlasting you are God.

You turn us back to dust and say:
'Turn back, O children of earth.'

For a thousand years in your sight are but as yesterday,
which passes like a watch in the night.   *Psalm 90.1-4*

One or more readings follows. The psalms may be used at the place of burial (see Note on page 44).

'O that my words were written down!
O that they were inscribed in a book!
O that with an iron pen and with lead
    they were engraved on a rock for ever!
For I know that my Redeemer lives,
    and that at the last he will stand upon the earth;
and after my skin has been thus destroyed,
then in my flesh I shall see God,
whom I shall see on my side,
    and my eyes shall behold, and not another.
My heart faints within me!'   *Job 19.23-27*

4   The Lord himself is my portion and my cup; ♦
     in your hands alone is my fortune.

5   My share has fallen in a fair land; ♦
     indeed, I have a goodly heritage.

6   I will bless the Lord who has given me counsel, ♦
     and in the night watches he instructs my heart.

7   I have set the Lord always before me; ♦
     he is at my right hand; I shall not fall.

8   Wherefore my heart is glad and my spirit rejoices; ♦
     my flesh also shall rest secure.

9   For you will not abandon my soul to Death, ♦
     nor suffer your faithful one to see the Pit.

10   You will show me the path of life;
         in your presence is the fullness of joy ♦
     and in your right hand are pleasures for evermore.   *Psalm 16.4-10*

1   O Lord, you have searched me out and known me; ♦
    you know my sitting down and my rising up;
        you discern my thoughts from afar.

2   You mark out my journeys and my resting place ♦
    and are acquainted with all my ways.

3   For there is not a word on my tongue, ♦
    but you, O Lord, know it altogether.

4   You encompass me behind and before ♦
    and lay your hand upon me.

5   Such knowledge is too wonderful for me, ♦
    so high that I cannot attain it.

6   Where can I go then from your spirit? ♦
    Or where can I flee from your presence?

7   If I climb up to heaven, you are there; ♦
    if I make the grave my bed, you are there also.

8   If I take the wings of the morning ♦
    and dwell in the uttermost parts of the sea,

9   Even there your hand shall lead me, ♦
    your right hand hold me fast.

10 If I say, 'Surely the darkness will cover me ♦
    and the light around me turn to night,'

11 Even darkness is no darkness with you;
        the night is as clear as the day; ♦
    darkness and light to you are both alike.

13 I thank you, for I am fearfully and wonderfully made; ♦
    marvellous are your works, my soul knows well.   *Psalm 139.1-11,13*

Someone will ask, 'How are the dead raised? With what kind of
body do they come?' Fool! What you sow does not come to life
unless it dies. And as for what you sow, you do not sow the body
that is to be, but a bare seed, perhaps of wheat or of some other
grain. But God gives it a body as he has chosen, and to each kind
of seed its own body.

So it is with the resurrection of the dead. What is sown is
perishable, what is raised is imperishable. It is sown in dishonour,
it is raised in glory. It is sown in weakness, it is raised in power.
It is sown a physical body, it is raised a spiritual body.

1 Corinthians 15.35-38, 42-44a

After these things, Joseph of Arimathea, who was a disciple of Jesus,
though a secret one because of his fear of the Jews, asked Pilate to
let him take away the body of Jesus. Pilate gave him permission; so
he came and removed his body. Nicodemus, who had at first come
to Jesus by night, also came, bringing a mixture of myrrh and aloes,
weighing about a hundred pounds. They took the body of Jesus and
wrapped it with the spices in linen cloths, according to the burial
custom of the Jews. Now there was a garden in the place where he
was crucified, and in the garden there was a new tomb in which no
one had ever been laid. And so, because it was the Jewish day of
Preparation, and the tomb was nearby, they laid Jesus there.

John 19.38-end

I saw no temple in the city, for its temple is the Lord God the
Almighty and the Lamb. And the city has no need of sun or moon to
shine on it, for the glory of God is its light, and its lamp is the Lamb.
The nations will walk by its light, and the kings of the earth will bring
their glory into it. Its gates will never be shut by day – and there will
be no night there. People will bring into it the glory and the honour
of the nations. But nothing unclean will enter it, nor anyone who
practises abomination or falsehood, but only those who are written
in the Lamb's book of life.

But the throne of God and of the Lamb will be in it, and his servants
will worship him; they will see his face, and his name will be on their
foreheads. And there will be no more night; they need no light of
lamp or sun, for the Lord God will be their light, and they will reign
for ever and ever.   *Revelation 21.22-end, 22.3b-5*

either

We have entrusted our *brother/sister* N to God's mercy,
and we now commit *his/her* mortal remains to the ground:
earth to earth, ashes to ashes, dust to dust:
in sure and certain hope of the resurrection to eternal life
through our Lord Jesus Christ,
who will transform our frail bodies
that they may be conformed to his glorious body,
who died, was buried, and rose again for us.
To him be glory for ever.

All **Amen.**

(or)

God our Father,
in loving care your hand has created us,
and as the potter fashions the clay
you have formed us in your image.
Through the Holy Spirit
you have breathed into us the gift of life.
In the sharing of love you have enriched our knowledge
    of you and of one another.
We claim your love today,
as we return these ashes to the ground
in sure and certain hope of the resurrection to eternal life.

The congregation may join with the minister in saying

All **Thanks be to God who gives us the victory**
through Jesus Christ our Lord. Amen.

The Lord's Prayer

As our Saviour taught us, so we pray

All **Our Father in heaven,
hallowed be your name,
your kingdom come,
your will be done,
on earth as in heaven.
Give us today our daily bread.
Forgive us our sins
as we forgive those who sin against us.
Lead us not into temptation
but deliver us from evil.
For the kingdom, the power,
and the glory are yours
now and for ever.
Amen.**

(or)

Let us pray with confidence as our Saviour has taught us

All **Our Father, who art in heaven,
hallowed be thy name;
thy kingdom come;
thy will be done;
on earth as it is in heaven.
Give us this day our daily bread.
And forgive us our trespasses,
as we forgive those who trespass against us.
And lead us not into temptation;
but deliver us from evil.
For thine is the kingdom,
the power and the glory,
for ever and ever.
Amen.**

Heavenly Father,
we thank you for all those whom we love but see no longer.
As we remember *N* in this place,
hold before us our beginning and our ending,
the dust from which we come
and the death to which we move,
with a firm hope in your eternal love and purposes for us,
in Jesus Christ our Lord.

All **Amen.**

Other prayers may be used, ending with

God of hope,
grant that we, with all who have believed in you,
may be united in the full knowledge of your love
and the unclouded vision of your glory;
through Jesus Christ our Lord.

All **Amen.**

The Dismissal

May the infinite and glorious Trinity,
the Father, the Son, and the Holy Spirit,
direct our life in good works,
and after our journey through this world
grant us eternal rest with all the saints.

All **Amen.**

Psalms

1   O Lord, rebuke me not in your wrath; ♦
    neither chasten me in your fierce anger.

2   Have mercy on me, Lord, for I am weak; ♦
    Lord, heal me, for my bones are racked.

3   My soul also shakes with terror; ♦
    how long, O Lord, how long?

4   Turn again, O Lord, and deliver my soul; ♦
    save me for your loving mercy's sake.

5   For in death no one remembers you; ♦
    and who can give you thanks in the grave?

6   I am weary with my groaning; ♦
    every night I drench my pillow
        and flood my bed with my tears.

7   My eyes are wasted with grief ♦
    and worn away because of all my enemies.

8   Depart from me, all you that do evil, ♦
    for the Lord has heard the voice of my weeping.

9   The Lord has heard my supplication; ♦
    the Lord will receive my prayer.

10 All my enemies shall be put to shame and confusion; ♦
    they shall suddenly turn back in their shame.

1   The Lord is my shepherd; ♦
therefore can I lack nothing.

2   He makes me lie down in green pastures ♦
and leads me beside still waters.

3   He shall refresh my soul ♦
and guide me in the paths of righteousness for his name's sake.

4   Though I walk through the valley of the shadow of death,
        I will fear no evil; ♦
for you are with me;
        your rod and your staff, they comfort me.

5   You spread a table before me
        in the presence of those who trouble me; ♦
you have anointed my head with oil
        and my cup shall be full.

6   Surely goodness and loving mercy shall follow me
        all the days of my life, ♦
and I will dwell in the house of the Lord for ever.

1   To you, O Lord, I lift up my soul;
        O my God, in you I trust; ♦
let me not be put to shame;
        let not my enemies triumph over me.

2   Let none who look to you be put to shame, ♦
but let the treacherous be shamed and frustrated.

3   Make me to know your ways, O Lord, ♦
and teach me your paths.

4   Lead me in your truth and teach me, ♦
for you are the God of my salvation;
        for you have I hoped all the day long.

5   Remember, Lord, your compassion and love, ♦
for they are from everlasting.

6   Remember not the sins of my youth
       or my transgressions, ♦
    but think on me in your goodness, O Lord,
       according to your steadfast love.

7   Gracious and upright is the Lord; ♦
    therefore shall he teach sinners in the way.

8   He will guide the humble in doing right ♦
    and teach his way to the lowly.

9   All the paths of the Lord are mercy and truth ♦
    to those who keep his covenant and his testimonies.

10   For your name's sake, O Lord, ♦
    be merciful to my sin, for it is great.

11   Who are those who fear the Lord? ♦
    Them will he teach in the way that they should choose.

12   Their soul shall dwell at ease ♦
    and their offspring shall inherit the land.

13   The hidden purpose of the Lord is for those who fear him ♦
    and he will show them his covenant.

14   My eyes are ever looking to the Lord, ♦
    for he shall pluck my feet out of the net.

15   Turn to me and be gracious to me, ♦
    for I am alone and brought very low.

16   The sorrows of my heart have increased; ♦
    O bring me out of my distress.

17   Look upon my adversity and misery ♦
    and forgive me all my sin.

18   Look upon my enemies, for they are many ♦
    and they bear a violent hatred against me.

19   O keep my soul and deliver me; ♦
    let me not be put to shame, for I have put my trust in you.

20   Let integrity and uprightness preserve me, ♦
    for my hope has been in you.

21   Deliver Israel, O God, ♦
    out of all his troubles.

1   The Lord is my light and my salvation;
        whom then shall I fear? ♦
    The Lord is the strength of my life;
        of whom then shall I be afraid?

2   When the wicked, even my enemies and my foes,
        came upon me to eat up my flesh, ♦
    they stumbled and fell.

3   Though a host encamp against me,
        my heart shall not be afraid, ♦
    and though there rise up war against me,
        yet will I put my trust in him.

4   One thing have I asked of the Lord
        and that alone I seek: ♦
    that I may dwell in the house of the Lord
        all the days of my life,

5   To behold the fair beauty of the Lord ♦
    and to seek his will in his temple.

6   For in the day of trouble
        he shall hide me in his shelter; ♦
    in the secret place of his dwelling shall he hide me
        and set me high upon a rock.

7   And now shall he lift up my head ♦
    above my enemies round about me;

8   Therefore will I offer in his dwelling an oblation
        with great gladness; ♦
    I will sing and make music to the Lord.

9   Hear my voice, O Lord, when I call; ♦
    have mercy upon me and answer me.

10   My heart tells of your word, 'Seek my face.' ♦
    Your face, Lord, will I seek.

11   Hide not your face from me, ♦
    nor cast your servant away in displeasure.

12   You have been my helper; ♦
    leave me not, neither forsake me, O God of my salvation.

13   Though my father and my mother forsake me, ♦
      the Lord will take me up.

14   Teach me your way, O Lord; ♦
      lead me on a level path,
            because of those who lie in wait for me.

15   Deliver me not into the will of my adversaries, ♦
      for false witnesses have risen up against me,
            and those who breathe out violence.

16   I believe that I shall see the goodness of the Lord ♦
      in the land of the living.

17   Wait for the Lord;
            be strong and he shall comfort your heart; ♦
      wait patiently for the Lord.

Psalm 32

1   Happy the one whose transgression is forgiven, ♦
      and whose sin is covered.

2   Happy the one to whom the Lord imputes no guilt, ♦
      and in whose spirit there is no guile.

3   For I held my tongue; ♦
      my bones wasted away
            through my groaning all the day long.

4   Your hand was heavy upon me day and night; ♦
      my moisture was dried up like the drought in summer.

5   Then I acknowledged my sin to you ♦
      and my iniquity I did not hide.

6   I said, 'I will confess my transgressions to the Lord,' ♦
      and you forgave the guilt of my sin.

7   Therefore let all the faithful make their prayers to you
            in time of trouble; ♦
      in the great water flood, it shall not reach them.

8   You are a place for me to hide in;
            you preserve me from trouble; ♦
      you surround me with songs of deliverance.

9   'I will instruct you and teach you
          in the way that you should go; ♦
     I will guide you with my eye.

10   'Be not like horse and mule which have no understanding; ♦
     whose mouths must be held with bit and bridle,
          or else they will not stay near you.'

11   Great tribulations remain for the wicked, ♦
     but mercy embraces those who trust in the Lord.

12   Be glad, you righteous, and rejoice in the Lord; ♦
     shout for joy, all who are true of heart.

Psalm 38

9   O Lord, you know all my desires ♦
     and my sighing is not hidden from you.

10   My heart is pounding, my strength has failed me; ♦
     the light of my eyes is gone from me.

11   My friends and companions stand apart from my affliction; ♦
     my neighbours stand afar off.

12   Those who seek after my life lay snares for me; ♦
     and those who would harm me whisper evil
          and mutter slander all the day long.

13   But I am like one who is deaf and hears not, ♦
     like one that is dumb, who does not open his mouth.

14   I have become like one who does not hear ♦
     and from whose mouth comes no retort.

15   For in you, Lord, have I put my trust; ♦
     you will answer me, O Lord my God.

16   For I said, 'Let them not triumph over me, ♦
     those who exult over me when my foot slips.'

17   Truly, I am on the verge of falling ♦
     and my pain is ever with me.

18   I will confess my iniquity ♦
     and be sorry for my sin.

19   Those that are my enemies without any cause are mighty, ♦
     and those who hate me wrongfully are many in number.

20   Those who repay evil for good are against me, ♦
      because the good is what I seek.

21   Forsake me not, O Lord; ♦
      be not far from me, O my God.

22   Make haste to help me, ♦
      O Lord of my salvation.

Psalm 42

1   As the deer longs for the water brooks, ♦
      so longs my soul for you, O God.

2   My soul is athirst for God, even for the living God; ♦
      when shall I come before the presence of God?

3   My tears have been my bread day and night, ♦
      while all day long they say to me, 'Where is now your God?'

4   Now when I think on these things, I pour out my soul: ♦
      how I went with the multitude
            and led the procession to the house of God,

5   With the voice of praise and thanksgiving, ♦
      among those who kept holy day.

6   *Why are you so full of heaviness, O my soul, ♦*
      and why are you so disquieted within me?

7   *O put your trust in God; ♦*
      for I will yet give him thanks,
            who is the help of my countenance, and my God.

8   My soul is heavy within me; ♦
      therefore I will remember you from the land of Jordan,
            and from Hermon and the hill of Mizar.

9   Deep calls to deep in the thunder of your waterfalls; ♦
      all your breakers and waves have gone over me.

10   The Lord will grant his loving-kindness in the daytime; ♦
      through the night his song will be with me,
            a prayer to the God of my life.

11   I say to God my rock,
            'Why have you forgotten me, ♦
      and why go I so heavily, while the enemy oppresses me?'

12   As they crush my bones, my enemies mock me; ♦
       while all day long they say to me, 'Where is now your God?'

13   *Why are you so full of heaviness, O my soul, ♦*
       and why are you so disquieted within me?

14   *O put your trust in God; ♦*
       for I will yet give him thanks,
             who is the help of my countenance, and my God.

Psalm 90

1   Lord, you have been our refuge ♦
       from one generation to another.

2   Before the mountains were brought forth,
             or the earth and the world were formed, ♦
       from everlasting to everlasting you are God.

3   You turn us back to dust and say: ♦
       'Turn back, O children of earth.'

4   For a thousand years in your sight are but as yesterday, ♦
       which passes like a watch in the night.

5   You sweep them away like a dream; ♦
       they fade away suddenly like the grass.

6   In the morning it is green and flourishes; ♦
       in the evening it is dried up and withered.

7   For we consume away in your displeasure; ♦
       we are afraid at your wrathful indignation.

8   You have set our misdeeds before you ♦
       and our secret sins in the light of your countenance.

9   When you are angry, all our days are gone; ♦
       our years come to an end like a sigh.

10   The days of our life are three score years and ten,
             or if our strength endures, even four score; ♦
       yet the sum of them is but labour and sorrow,
             for they soon pass away and we are gone.

11   Who regards the power of your wrath ♦
       and your indignation like those who fear you?

12   So teach us to number our days ♦
       that we may apply our hearts to wisdom.

13   Turn again, O Lord; how long will you delay? ♦
      Have compassion on your servants.

14   Satisfy us with your loving-kindness in the morning, ♦
      that we may rejoice and be glad all our days.

15   Give us gladness for the days you have afflicted us, ♦
      and for the years in which we have seen adversity.

16   Show your servants your works, ♦
      and let your glory be over their children.

17   May the gracious favour of the Lord our God be upon us; ♦
      prosper our handiwork; O prosper the work of our hands.

Psalm 116

1   I love the Lord,
          for he has heard the voice of my supplication; ♦
      because he inclined his ear to me
          on the day I called to him.

2   The snares of death encompassed me;
          the pains of hell took hold of me; ♦
      by grief and sorrow was I held.

3   Then I called upon the name of the Lord: ♦
      'O Lord, I beg you, deliver my soul.'

4   Gracious is the Lord and righteous; ♦
      our God is full of compassion.

5   The Lord watches over the simple; ♦
      I was brought very low and he saved me.

6   Turn again to your rest, O my soul, ♦
      for the Lord has been gracious to you.

7   For you have delivered my soul from death, ♦
      my eyes from tears and my feet from falling.

8   I will walk before the Lord ♦
      in the land of the living.

9   I believed that I should perish
          for I was sorely troubled; ♦
      and I said in my alarm,
          'Everyone is a liar.'

10   How shall I repay the Lord ♦
      for all the benefits he has given to me?

11   I will lift up the cup of salvation ♦
      and call upon the name of the Lord.

12   I will fulfil my vows to the Lord ♦
      in the presence of all his people.

13   Precious in the sight of the Lord ♦
      is the death of his faithful servants.

14   O Lord, I am your servant, ♦
      your servant, the child of your handmaid;
            you have freed me from my bonds.

15   I will offer to you a sacrifice of thanksgiving ♦
      and call upon the name of the Lord.

16   I will fulfil my vows to the Lord ♦
      in the presence of all his people,

17   In the courts of the house of the Lord, ♦
      in the midst of you, O Jerusalem.
            Alleluia.

Psalm 118

4   Let those who fear the Lord proclaim, ♦
      'His mercy endures for ever.'

5   In my constraint I called to the Lord; ♦
      the Lord answered and set me free.

6   The Lord is at my side; I will not fear; ♦
      what can flesh do to me?

7   With the Lord at my side as my saviour, ♦
      I shall see the downfall of my enemies.

8   It is better to take refuge in the Lord ♦
      than to put any confidence in flesh.

9   It is better to take refuge in the Lord ♦
      than to put any confidence in princes.

10   All the nations encompassed me, ♦
      but by the name of the Lord I drove them back.

11   They hemmed me in, they hemmed me in on every side, ♦
      but by the name of the Lord I drove them back.

12   They swarmed about me like bees;
          they blazed like fire among thorns, ♦
      but by the name of the Lord I drove them back.

13   Surely, I was thrust to the brink, ♦
      but the Lord came to my help.

14   The Lord is my strength and my song, ♦
      and he has become my salvation.

15   Joyful shouts of salvation ♦
      sound from the tents of the righteous:

16   'The right hand of the Lord does mighty deeds;
          the right hand of the Lord raises up; ♦
      the right hand of the Lord does mighty deeds.'

17   I shall not die, but live ♦
      and declare the works of the Lord.

18   The Lord has punished me sorely, ♦
      but he has not given me over to death.

19   Open to me the gates of righteousness, ♦
      that I may enter and give thanks to the Lord.

20   This is the gate of the Lord; ♦
      the righteous shall enter through it.

21   I will give thanks to you, for you have answered me ♦
      and have become my salvation.

22   The stone which the builders rejected ♦
      has become the chief cornerstone.

23   This is the Lord's doing, ♦
      and it is marvellous in our eyes.

24   This is the day that the Lord has made; ♦
      we will rejoice and be glad in it.

25   Come, O Lord, and save us we pray. ♦
      Come, Lord, send us now prosperity.

26   Blessed is he who comes in the name of the Lord; ♦
      we bless you from the house of the Lord.

27   The Lord is God; he has given us light; ♦
link the pilgrims with cords
          right to the horns of the altar.

28   You are my God and I will thank you; ♦
you are my God and I will exalt you.

29   O give thanks to the Lord, for he is good; ♦
his mercy endures for ever.

1   I lift up my eyes to the hills; ♦
from where is my help to come?

2   My help comes from the Lord, ♦
the maker of heaven and earth.

3   He will not suffer your foot to stumble; ♦
he who watches over you will not sleep.

4   Behold, he who keeps watch over Israel ♦
shall neither slumber nor sleep.

5   The Lord himself watches over you; ♦
the Lord is your shade at your right hand,

6   So that the sun shall not strike you by day, ♦
neither the moon by night.

7   The Lord shall keep you from all evil; ♦
it is he who shall keep your soul.

8   The Lord shall keep watch over your going out
          and your coming in, ♦
from this time forth for evermore.

1   O Lord, you have searched me out and known me; ♦
you know my sitting down and my rising up;
   you discern my thoughts from afar.

2   You mark out my journeys and my resting place ♦
and are acquainted with all my ways.

3   For there is not a word on my tongue, ♦
but you, O Lord, know it altogether.

4   You encompass me behind and before ♦
and lay your hand upon me.

5   Such knowledge is too wonderful for me, ♦
so high that I cannot attain it.

6   Where can I go then from your spirit? ♦
Or where can I flee from your presence?

7   If I climb up to heaven, you are there; ♦
if I make the grave my bed, you are there also.

8   If I take the wings of the morning ♦
and dwell in the uttermost parts of the sea,

9   Even there your hand shall lead me, ♦
your right hand hold me fast.

10   If I say, 'Surely the darkness will cover me ♦
and the light around me turn to night,'

11   Even darkness is no darkness with you;
   the night is as clear as the day; ♦
darkness and light to you are both alike.

12   For you yourself created my inmost parts; ♦
you knit me together in my mother's womb.

13   I thank you, for I am fearfully and wonderfully made; ♦
marvellous are your works, my soul knows well.

14   My frame was not hidden from you, ♦
when I was made in secret
   and woven in the depths of the earth.

15   Your eyes beheld my form, as yet unfinished; ♦
already in your book were all my members written,

16   As day by day they were fashioned ♦
        when as yet there was none of them.

17   How deep are your counsels to me, O God! ♦
        How great is the sum of them!

18   If I count them, they are more in number than the sand, ♦
        and at the end, I am still in your presence.

19   O that you would slay the wicked, O God, ♦
        that the bloodthirsty might depart from me!

20   They speak against you with wicked intent; ♦
        your enemies take up your name for evil.

21   Do I not oppose those, O Lord, who oppose you? ♦
        Do I not abhor those who rise up against you?

22   I hate them with a perfect hatred; ♦
        they have become my own enemies also.

23   Search me out, O God, and know my heart; ♦
        try me and examine my thoughts.

24   See if there is any way of wickedness in me ♦
        and lead me in the way everlasting.

Canticles

A Song of the Redeemer

Refrain:

All   **Proclaim the time of the Lord's favour,
and comfort all who grieve.**

1   The Spirit of the Lord is upon me, ♦
because he has anointed me.

2   He has sent me to bind up the brokenhearted, ♦
to announce release from darkness for the prisoners,

3   To proclaim the time of the Lord's favour, ♦
and to comfort all who grieve,

4   To give them oil of gladness instead of mourners' tears, ♦
a garment of splendour for the heavy heart.

5   They will be called trees of righteousness, ♦
planted by the Lord for his praise.

6   For God shall make his righteousness and praise ♦
blossom before all the nations.

7   Buildings long in ruins will be rebuilt ♦
and the desolate cities restored.

8   And you shall be called the Redeemed of the Lord, ♦
a city no longer forsaken.   *Isaiah 61.1-3,11b,4; 62.12*

Glory to the Father, and to the Son
and to the Holy Spirit;
as it was in the beginning is now
and shall be for ever. Amen.

The Song of Manasseh

All   **Full of compassion and mercy and love
is God, the Most High, the Almighty.**

1   O Lord almighty and God of our forebears, ♦
you who made heaven and earth in all their glory:

2   All things tremble with awe at your presence, ♦
before your great and mighty power.

3   Immeasurable and unsearchable is your promise of mercy, ♦
for you are God, Most High.

4   You are full of compassion and very merciful, ♦
and you relent at human suffering.

5   O God, according to your great goodness, ♦
you have promised repentance and forgiveness
    to those who have sinned against you.

6   The sins I have committed against you ♦
are more in number than the sands of the sea.

7   I am not worthy to look up and see the heavens, ♦
because of my many sins and iniquities.

8   And now my heart bows before you, ♦
imploring your kindness upon me.

9   I have sinned, O God, I have sinned, ♦
and I acknowledge my transgressions.

10   Unworthy as I am, I know that you will save me, ♦
according to your great mercy.

11   For all the host of heaven sings your praise, ♦
and your glory is for ever and ever.

Manasseh 1a,2,4,6,7,9a,9c,11,12,14b,15b

Glory to the Father, and to the Son
and to the Holy Spirit;
as it was in the beginning is now
and shall be for ever. Amen.

A Song of the Righteous

All   **God has found the righteous worthy
and their hope is of immortality.**

1   The souls of the righteous are in the hand of God ♦
and no torment will ever touch them.

2   In the eyes of the foolish, they seem to have died; ♦
but they are at peace.

3   For though, in the sight of others, they were punished, ♦
their hope is of immortality.

4   Having been disciplined a little,
they will receive great good, ♦
because God tested them and found them worthy.

5   Like gold in the furnace, God tried them ♦
and, like a sacrificial burnt offering, accepted them.

6   In the time of their visitation, they will shine forth ♦
and will run like sparks through the stubble.

7   They will govern nations and rule over peoples ♦
and God will reign over them for ever.   *Wisdom 3.1,2a,3b-8*

Glory to the Father, and to the Son
and to the Holy Spirit;
as it was in the beginning is now
and shall be for ever. Amen.

Nunc dimittis (The Song of Simeon)

All   **Awake may we watch with Christ:**
asleep may we rest in peace.

1   Now, Lord, you let your servant go in peace: ♦
your word has been fulfilled.

2   My own eyes have seen the salvation ♦
which you have prepared in the sight of every people;

3   A light to reveal you to the nations ♦
and the glory of your people Israel.   *Luke 2.29-32*

Glory to the Father, and to the Son
and to the Holy Spirit;
as it was in the beginning is now
and shall be for ever. Amen.

1   Lord, now lettest thou thy servant depart in peace :
according to thy word.

2   For mine eyes have seen :
thy salvation;

3   Which thou hast prepared :
before the face of all people;

4   To be a light to lighten the Gentiles :
and to be the glory of thy people Israel.   *Luke 2.29-32*

Glory be to the Father, and to the Son :
and to the Holy Ghost;
as it was in the beginning, is now, and ever shall be :
world without end. Amen.

A Song of the Justified

All **We are justified by faith,**
we have peace with God through our Lord Jesus Christ.

1 God reckons as righteous those who believe, ♦
who believe in him who raised Jesus from the dead;

2 For Christ was handed over to death for our sins, ♦
and raised to life for our justification.

3 Since we are justified by faith, ♦
we have peace with God through our Lord Jesus Christ.

4 Through Christ we have gained access
to the grace in which we stand, ♦
and rejoice in our hope of the glory of God.

5 We even exult in our sufferings, ♦
for suffering produces endurance,

6 And endurance brings hope, ♦
and our hope is not in vain,

7 Because God's love has been poured into our hearts, ♦
through the Holy Spirit, given to us.

8 God proves his love for us: ♦
while we were yet sinners Christ died for us.

9 Since we have been justified by his death, ♦
how much more shall we be saved from God's wrath.

10 Therefore, we exult in God through our Lord Jesus Christ, ♦
in whom we have now received our reconciliation.

Romans 4.24,25; 5.1-5,8,9,11

Glory to the Father, and to the Son
and to the Holy Spirit;
as it was in the beginning is now
and shall be for ever. Amen.

A Song of God's Children

All **The Spirit of the Father,
who raises Christ Jesus from the dead,
gives life to the people of God.**

1   The law of the Spirit of life in Christ Jesus ♦
has set us free from the law of sin and death.

2   All who are led by the Spirit of God are children of God; ♦
for we have received the Spirit that enables us to cry, 'Abba, Father'.

3   The Spirit himself bears witness that we are children of God ♦
and if God's children, then heirs of God;

4   If heirs of God, then fellow-heirs with Christ; ♦
since we suffer with him now, that we may be glorified with him.

5   These sufferings that we now endure ♦
are not worth comparing to the glory that shall be revealed.

6   For the creation waits with eager longing ♦
for the revealing of the children of God.   *Romans 8.2,14,15b-19*

Glory to the Father, and to the Son
and to the Holy Spirit;
as it was in the beginning is now
and shall be for ever. Amen.

A Song of Faith

Refrain:

All   **God raised Christ from the dead,**
the Lamb without spot or stain.

1   Blessed be the God and Father ♦
of our Lord Jesus Christ!

2   By his great mercy we have been born anew to a living hope ♦
through the resurrection of Jesus Christ from the dead,

3   Into an inheritance that is imperishable, undefiled and unfading, ♦
kept in heaven for you,

4   Who are being protected by the power of God
through faith for a salvation ♦
ready to be revealed in the last time.

5   You were ransomed from the futile ways of your ancestors ♦
not with perishable things like silver or gold

6   But with the precious blood of Christ ♦
like that of a lamb without spot or stain.

7   Through him we have confidence in God,
who raised him from the dead and gave him glory, ♦
so that your faith and hope are set on God.   *1 Peter 1.3-5,18,19,21*

Glory to the Father and to the Son
and to the Holy Spirit;
as it was in the beginning is now
and shall be for ever. Amen.

A Song of the Redeemed

All **Salvation belongs to our God,**
who will guide us to springs of living water.

1 Behold, a great multitude ♦
which no one could number,

2 From every nation,
from all tribes and peoples and tongues, ♦
standing before the throne and the Lamb.

3 They were clothed in white robes
and had palms in their hands, ♦
and they cried with a loud voice, saying,

4 'Salvation belongs to our God
who sits on the throne, ♦
and to the Lamb.'

5 These are they
who have come out of the great tribulation, ♦
they have washed their robes
and made them white in the blood of the Lamb;

6 Therefore they stand before the throne of God, ♦
whom they serve day and night within the temple.

7 And the One who sits upon the throne ♦
will shelter them with his presence.

8 They shall never again feel hunger or thirst, ♦
the sun shall not strike them,
nor any scorching heat.

9 For the Lamb at the heart of the throne ♦
will be their Shepherd,

10 He will guide them to springs of living water, ♦
and God will wipe away every tear from their eyes.

Revelation 7.9,10,14b-17

To the One who sits on the throne and to the Lamb
be blessing and honour and glory and might,
for ever and ever. Amen.

A Song of the Lamb

All **Let us rejoice and exult
and give glory and homage to our God.**

1   Salvation and glory and power belong to our God, ◆
     whose judgements are true and just.

2   Praise our God, all you his servants, ◆
     all who fear him, both small and great.

3   The Lord our God, the Almighty, reigns: ◆
     let us rejoice and exult and give him the glory.

4   For the marriage of the Lamb has come ◆
     and his bride has made herself ready.

5   Blessed are those who are invited ◆
     to the wedding banquet of the Lamb.

Revelation 19.1b,2b,5b,6b,7,9b

To the One who sits on the throne and to the Lamb
be blessing and honour and glory and might,
    for ever and ever. Amen.

A Song of St Anselm

All   **Gather your little ones to you, O God,
as a hen gathers her brood to protect them.**

1   Jesus, like a mother you gather your people to you; ♦
you are gentle with us as a mother with her children.

2   Often you weep over our sins and our pride, ♦
tenderly you draw us from hatred and judgement.

3   You comfort us in sorrow and bind up our wounds, ♦
in sickness you nurse us, and with pure milk you feed us.

4   Jesus, by your dying we are born to new life; ♦
by your anguish and labour we come forth in joy.

5   Despair turns to hope through your sweet goodness; ♦
through your gentleness we find comfort in fear.

6   Your warmth gives life to the dead, ♦
your touch makes sinners righteous.

7   Lord Jesus, in your mercy heal us; ♦
in your love and tenderness remake us.

8   In your compassion bring grace and forgiveness, ♦
for the beauty of heaven may your love prepare us.

from Anselm of Canterbury

Glory to the Father, and to the Son
and to the Holy Spirit;
as it was in the beginning is now
and shall be for ever. Amen.

Authorization

The following services and other material in *Common Worship: Pastoral Services* are authorized pursuant to Canon B 2 of the Canons of the Church of England for use until further resolution of the General Synod:

- The Outline Order for Funerals
- The Funeral Service
- The Funeral Service within a Celebration of Holy Communion
- The Blessing of a Grave
- The Burial of Ashes
- Prayers of Entrusting and Commending
- Bible Readings and Psalms for Use at Funeral and Memorial Services
- Nunc dimittis
- General Rules for Regulating Authorized Forms of Service

The Canticles (other than the Nunc dimittis and Some Texts which may be used by the Minister) have been commended by the House of Bishops of the General Synod pursuant to Canon B 2 of the Canons of the Church of England and is published with the agreement of the House.

Under Canon B 4 it is open to each bishop to authorize, if he sees fit, the form of service to be used within his diocese. He may specify that the services shall be those commended by the House, or that a diocesan form of them shall be used. If the bishop gives no directions in this matter the priest remains free, subject to the terms of Canon B 5, to make use of the services as commended by the House.

Acknowledgements

The publisher gratefully acknowledges permission to reproduce copyright material in this book. Every effort has been made to trace and contact copyright holders. If there are any inadvertent omissions we apologize to those concerned and undertake to include suitable acknowledgements in all future editions.

Published sources include the following:

Cambridge University Press: Extracts (and adapted extracts) from *The Book of Common Prayer*, the rights in which are vested in the Crown, are reproduced by permission of the Crown's Patentee, Cambridge University Press.

The Division of Christian Education of the National Council of Churches in the USA: Unless otherwise stated, Scripture quotations are from *The New Revised Standard Version of the Bible,* copyright © 1989 by the Division of Christian Education of the National Council of Churches in the USA. Used by permission. All rights reserved.

Thanks are also due to the following for permission to reproduce copyright material:

The Anglican Church in Aotearoa, New Zealand and Polynesia: p. 6 the alternative opening prayer, prayer at the time of death ('N, go forth from this world: in the love of God the Father …'; p. 42). Taken/adapted from *A New Zealand Prayer Book – He Karikia Mihinare O Aotearoa,* copyright © The Church of the Province of New Zealand 1989.

The English Language Liturgical Consultation: The Lord's Prayer and the Nunc dimittis (p. 69 top) prepared by the English Language Liturgical Consultation, based on (or excerpted from) *Praying Together,* copyright © ELLC 1988.

The International Commission on English in the Liturgy: the Collect
(p.8). English translation based on (or excerpted from) *The Roman
Missal*, copyright © 1973 International Committee on English in the
Liturgy (ICEL). Prayers of entrusting and commending ('Lord Jesus,
our Redeemer …', p. 39 and '*N* has fallen asleep in the peace of
Christ …', p. 39). Based on (or excerpted from) the *Order of Christian
Funerals*, copyright © 1985 ICEL. All rights reserved.

The Episcopal Church in the USA: 'Into your hands, O merciful
Saviour …' (p. 42) from *The Book of Common Prayer* according to the
use of the Episcopal Church of the USA, 1979. The ECUSA Prayer
Book is not subject to copyright.

The European Province of the Society of St Francis: 'God of all
consolation …' (p.6) from *Celebrating Common Prayer*, copyright
© The Society of St Francis European Province 1992 and 1996.

Grove Books: Ending 72 (p. 40) from *Liturgy and Death*
(Grove Books, 1974) © Trevor Lloyd.